Luiz Antonio Vargas Pinto

Real-time operating system in a microcontroller environment

Luiz Antonio Vargas Pinto

Real-time operating system in a microcontroller environment

The Automation Connection

ScienciaScripts

Imprint

Any brand names and product names mentioned in this book are subject to trademark, brand or patent protection and are trademarks or registered trademarks of their respective holders. The use of brand names, product names, common names, trade names, product descriptions etc. even without a particular marking in this work is in no way to be construed to mean that such names may be regarded as unrestricted in respect of trademark and brand protection legislation and could thus be used by anyone.

Cover image: www.ingimage.com

This book is a translation from the original published under ISBN 978-620-2-40576-8.

Publisher:
Sciencia Scripts
is a trademark of
International Book Market Service Ltd., member of OmniScriptum Publishing Group
17 Meldrum Street, Beau Bassin 71504, Mauritius
Printed at: see last page
ISBN: 978-620-3-39299-9

Copyright © Luiz Antonio Vargas Pinto
Copyright © 2021 International Book Market Service Ltd., member of OmniScriptum Publishing Group

DEDICATION

To my wife for her patience in all the moments that I abstained from my family duties during my studies and to those who directly or indirectly contributed to the realization of this work.

ACKNOWLEDGMENT

To God first, to my family for their patience, and to all the professors at ESAB who supported me and cleared up doubts with patience.

I also thank those anonymous heroes who free the use of software to all those who want to learn. Thanks to Prof. Caribe Zampirolli de Souza and special thanks to Prof. Ma Janaina Costa Binda for her patience, support and vote of confidence.

"Something I have learned in a long life:
all our science, measured against reality,
is primitive and childish - and yet it is the
most precious thing we have."

Albert Einstein

SUMMARY

Themain objective of this work is to develop an RTC - Real Timer Clock system in process control equipment with microcontrollers from the ATMEL family (AT89S8253) or, at least, to develop a new approach in microcontroller programming, optimizing the use of their internal resources. To this end, we intend to study an industrial process to understand how a real-time system should adapt to this reality; to study a safe latency time, since the operating system must handle with a safe margin the times of the quantities involved. The development of a prototype of a Real Time Operating System to serve processes and obtain control. As a result of this study, it is expected to improve the use of microcontroller resources and the way programmers interact with the reality of industrialcontrol processes.

Keywords: microcontroller. operating system. real-time. industrial process

SUMMARY

1. INTRODUCTION

Is it possible to improve process safety and quality using microcontrollers operating with real-time architecture?

The main goal is to develop an RTC - Real Timer Clock system in process control equipment with microcontrollers from the ATMEL (AT89S8253) family.

No less important is it:

a) Study an industrial process to understand how a real-time system should fit into this reality;

b) Study a safe latency time, since the operating system must handle the times of the quantities involved with a safe margin;

c) Develop the prototype of a Real-Time Operating System to handle the process and local control of the device and evaluate its performance .

One candefinethe methodology employedby two methods suggestedinan adaptation of Richardson (1999, p. 326-327).

a) This is a historical research, in which the aim is to understand the phenomenon of basic industrial processes in order to better understand the "time" effect.

b) It is also an exploratory research because it intends to understand the space occupied by processes and the control with local microcontroller measuring the effect of its action on the process

However, the explanatory method that best fits this research is action research because it intends to conceptualize a real-time system; conceptualize the microcontroller structure and its application environment since it has many limitations - the universe is restricted.

Microcontroller environments are processing-rich and at the same time limited in memory space. This suggests that their application should be limited to small automation projects only. However, no less usual is the need for applications in process automation. The most important question should be whether there is application for microcontrollers for this need. For this to be possible the implementation of PID algorithms is the way to go.

To achieve this goal it is necessary to operate in Real-Time, and the limitations are: little program memory and little RAM. This makes it evident that the device's own limitation prevents the implementation of sophisticated algorithms, but does not prevent a discrete form of processing. In fact, more than just this, the result depends much more on further studies in control than on the limitation of the microcontroller. But this is also beyond the scope of this paper.

If somehow it is not possible to reach the extreme of control, at least one can initially direct the study to a proposal for real-time operation.

The rapid evolution of computer systems providing practically infinite resources - with emphasis on memories that at each generation have greater capacity and smaller size; photonic, quantum processors, etc.. - allows more and more comfortable programming for the programmer, but not everything is like that. In industrial environments, organization and simplicity are indispensable. In this environment, memory space is extremely limited and microcontrollers are designed for distributed or localized automation. And here computational procedures have felt little of the weather. Adjusting new programmers in a limited environment is the challenge. Here resource management is very important.

In addition, industrial processes require real-time service, which creates a great need for serial communication to distribute microcontrollers throughout the process with localized actuation.

The studies show that sequential tasks typical of time-sharing operating systems - introduced by Control Data Corporation (SCOPE OS) in the 1960s for batch processing and which later developed MACE OS for time-sharing - are not suitable in processes that behave randomly in their service requests.

The objective of this work is to develop a study and a prototype of a Real Time Operating System to be used in microcontroller-managed equipment, making it capable of serving more than a single process or at least, by the fact of managing resources, develop a new way of programming that enables programmers to have a more rigid and organized way of processing.

To this end, a study will be made of the parts surrounding the process such as the history of microprocessors, microcontrollers, real-time operating systems, process control and responses, and the study of timing and its effects on the behavior of the real-time kernel.

2. THEORY

2.1. HISTORY

Since the invention of the computer in the 1940s by Dr. John Von Neumman's team, the ENIAC[1] , much has been discussed about how and what is the best way to program it (VALLE 2010). Or better yet, about how it will have control over its peripherals.

It was quickly realized that the computer core was extremely faster than previously thought, particularly when it came to comparing it to humans in their everyday tasks.

Even though programming it was a very time-consuming task, that is, its programming, and even though it was extremely complex, the results were surprising. And what attracted the most attention was that, besides the programming difficulty, it was only possible to execute a single program at a time, so that the idle time of the utilization process itself made it expensive and of little use.

Between 1955 and 1965 batch processing (BATCH) was introduced, which was nothing more than a sequence of programs to be executed, i.e. one at a time, from start to finish. But there were still gaps of unused time.

In 1961 the MIT - Massachusetts Institute of Technology presented the "Compatible Time-Sharing System (CTSS)" which consisted of a computer that was accessed by multiple users through several terminals. This divided the time into equal packages (quotas) for all the processes that were executed in the computers of the time, which in a way allowed more than one program to be executed "at the same time", reducing the idleness of the computer (MCCARTHY 1983).

Around this same time, in mid-1958, studies revealed that the interrupt method could evolve a great deal, so much so as to influence new generations of computers.

Considering that the 4004 microprocessor from Intel© released in 1971 did not have any interrupt handling proposals built-in, it can be considered that such processes were much more complex in dates prior to 1971(INTEL CORPORATION 2013).

In April 1974 Intel©s 8080 microprocessor was released running at 2 MHz and incorporated interrupt handling. This suggests at least that computers built after this date that incorporated interrupt handling were leveraged by making operating systems much more efficient and compact than existing ones (INTELCORPORATION2013). It is not the scope of this monograph a detailed study of the computer models that have used these concepts in their operating system .

---

[1] The ENIAC Electronic Numerical Integrator And Computer implemented the first version of stored program as opposed to externally configured with wires

Although IBM© - International Business Machines nicknamed "Big Blue" for adopting blue as its official corporate color, had dominated the computer market for a long time even before the advent of the transistor, the computer market underwent strong changes such as the birth of a new family of computers known as "home computers" with Apple© Computers Inc. launching its Apple Computer using the 6502 microcontroller from Motorola©.

The operating system CP/M Control Program for Microcomputers originally created for Intel 8080/85 microcomputers by Gary Kildall of Digital Research©, Inc. and confined to single-tasking on 8-bit processors with no more than 64 Kbytes of memory, was adopted by the Z-80 microprocessor from Zilog©, a company created basically by Intel dissidents, and took a large part of the microcomputer operating systems on the market and introduced one of the most famous operating systems of the era of 8-bit processors (GUIMARÃES 2010).

Although it introduced later versions where it added variants for multiusers and migrated to 16-bit processors it did not survive the onslaught of the recent MS-DOS© that was introduced by Microsoft© Corporation - a new company on the market whose founders were Paul Allen and William Henry Gates III, Bill Gates .

Since then, operating systems have thrived. And they have generated roots that have spread into all processed systems. Computers are the perfect example of the sequence of these events.

2.2. MICROCONTROLLERS

Released in 1977, Intel©'s 8051 is a so-called "computer on a chip". While the computer market followed its course to what we have nowadays, it became essential to define the difference between microprocessors and microcontrollers (SILVA JR 1999).

Microprocessors follow a basic structure known as "Von Neumann" and for this reason have a high processing capacity. They are small, fast, process large amounts of information (audio and video) among others, which is why they are suitable for computers. Due to its constructive characteristics, all memory and peripherals are external to the CPU, which is basically a ULA - Logical and Arithmetic Unit (SILVA JR 1999).

Microcontrollers on the other hand follow the "Harvard" structure. For this reason they are small, not so fast - and there is no reason why, as will be explained later - and process limited amounts of information. And because of its construction characteristics, all memory and peripherals are internal to the chip, which has earned it the title "computer on a single chip". For example, it has RAM, FlashROM, Timer/Counter, Interrupt handling, serial communication (UART) among other features. Because of these differences the microcontroller structure is treated as

MPU differently from the microprocessors called CPU, and for this reason from now on references to microcontrollers will be referred to as MCU - Microcontroller Central Unit (SILVA JR 1999).

There are numerous applications which do not need as much processing and/or speed, and which require as little space as possible. For these, in many applications 8085 microprocessors from Intel© and Zilog©'s Z-80 have been used. However, given the characteristics presented, microcontrollers are better suited for these applications - basically because of the physical space and resources they have inside the chip. Since then the rate of use of microcontrollers has grown steadily, as they are already present in appliances, vehicles, aircraft and industrial control equipment such as PLCs - Programmable Logic Controllers (SILVA JR 1999).

3. THE INDUSTRIAL PROCESS

An industrial process is defined as a series of physical implementations that involve storage, drive, and interconnection between solid devices such as tanks and silos whose purpose is to obtain some final product in the controlled operation of these elements. For example, one can cite pressure and temperature control in fuel pipes (DORF 2009).

Under the action of control and disturbances, a process responds on a time scale in the manner shown in figure 1:

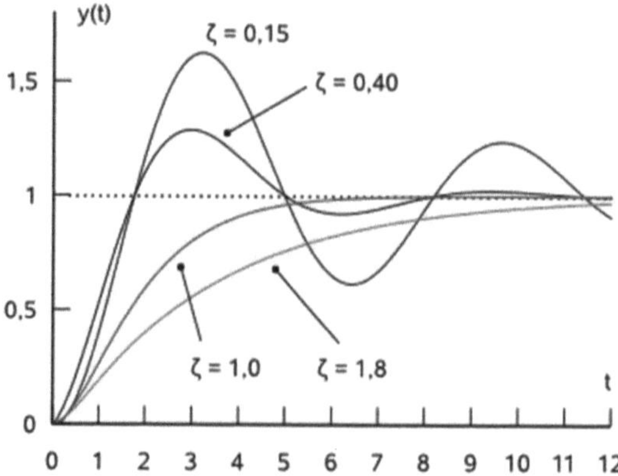

Figure 1: Process response in time

Source: www.mspc.eng.br

The Greek letterζ1 show us how a process behaves depending on the type of damping (BENTO 1989).

As it is not in the scope of this monograph, the study of the so-called 1st and 2nd degree systems will not be treated briefly, but with the exception of the observation of the effects of the time of action of the process and the reaction to external events.

It should also be remembered that the damping factor ζis used in the analysis of 2nd order systems, therefore, given its complexity, and in our case, for reasons of time, an attempt will be made to expose the system only under the action of variations restricted to 1st order systems (whose characteristics are simpler) that can be considered as those with $\zeta = 1$ as can be seen in the curve in red because these processes have a very slow response to external events (BENTO 1989).

15

In general, processes usually have the response to change depicted in figure 2.

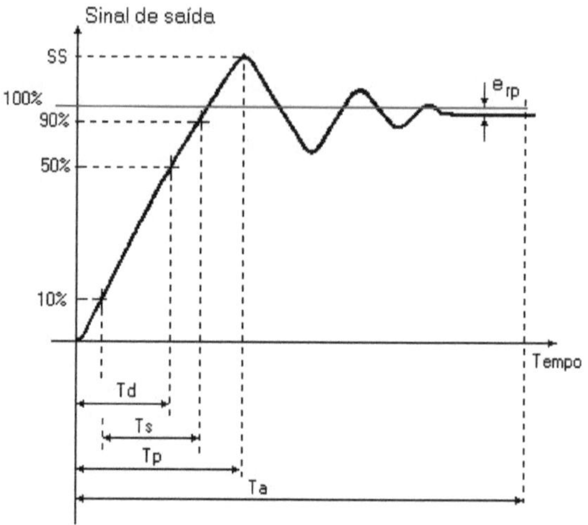

Figure 2: Process response to change

Source: Bento (1993)

with the following considerations (BENTO 1989 p56):

a) (Td) **delay time**: time required for the response to first reach 50% of the final value;

b) (Ts) **rise time**: time required for the response to go from 10 to 90% of its final value;

c) (Tp) **peak instant**: time required for the response to first reach the over-signal peak;

d) (SS) **oversignal**: is the maximum percentage that the response reaches with respect to the final signal;

e) (Ta) **settling time**: time required for the response signal to settle into its final value.

f) (eRP) **Steady state error**: is the residue that remains between the desired value and the obtained value;

4. REAL-TIME SYSTEMS

As a starting point it is necessary to study some definitions of the meanings of Real Time. Technically two classes of Real Time are established: Class A and Class B (MAGALHÃES 1986).

a) Class A: Refers to online processes, cases where people usually interact with a computerized system. It is typical in ticket purchases at terminals

b) Class B: They appear in industrial processes. Here the procedures must attend external events to the computerized system and must respect priority and have a defined time for response, not accepting the breaking of these criteria under penalty of serious disasters and/or accidents

In class A systems, time can be treated in a varied way since it is tolerant to this fact, which is usually not acceptable in class B systems; and it is precisely here that the system is intended to be built (MAGALHÃES1986).

Although some literature still differs a little on the definition of Real Time for class A, this is a fact that is not the scope of this work. For Magalhaes (1986, p.1), "[...] the end goal is a process... translated by the management of interruptions, and associated with the management of these interruptions, there is priority, meaning that the most important task needs to be served within the associated time constraint"

For its full functionality, instead of simply having the program codes, you have the programs allocated in program memory (flashrom) inside a capsule of codes known as a Task, which is described in chapter 2.41 .

A kernel manages the tasks that will use the MPU by alternating its allocation address and changing the contents of the registers in use causing the MPU to "think" that it is still executing the same codes abstracting from the real meaning of these codes (BBI 1986).

Possibly there will be a higher consumption of program memory, which has encouraged the use of more powerful microcontrollers, at least with DIP 40 (Dual In-Line Package) and that have more memory.

The Intel MCU family was adopted for having a dynamic stack pointer suitable for this type of procedure. In particular, the AT89S8253 MCU from Atmel© has, in addition to this stack pointer feature, a program memory with 12KB of FlashRom, 256 bytes of RAM and 2KB of EEPROM (INTEL CORPORATION 2013).

5. REAL-TIME SYSTEM STRUCTURE

5.1. Task Context Block

The basics of a real-time structure could be established by defining what is called a Task (MAGALHÃES 1986). Tasks are the microprograms that will act on the microcontroller, and in order to have control over each task that is occupying the microcontroller, these must have their structure defined for the context of the real-time core as a <u>Task Context Block</u> or simply **BCT** shown in figure 3.

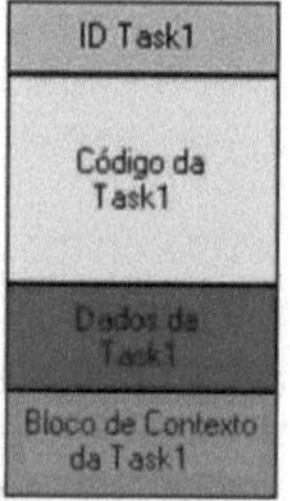

Figure 3: Task Context Block

Source: Elaborated by the author (2013)

ID - This is the task identifier. And it takes only one byte that identifies each task in use - each has its own ID.

Code - This is of varying length and truly corresponds to the code of a micro-program that will use the MPU.

Data - These are the bytes in internal RAM belonging to the Task in question. The number of bytes is also of variable size depending on the Task.

Context Block - Is of fixed size and is a copy of the registers that the Task would be using at the moment it was suspended so that it can return exactly to what it was doing at the moment of suspension

The set of these elements is called the <u>Task Context Block</u> and each task has its BCT distributed as shown in figure 4. This would be an overview of the distribution of tasks (Task), which of course will be as small as possible. Each one is a program with all its parts.

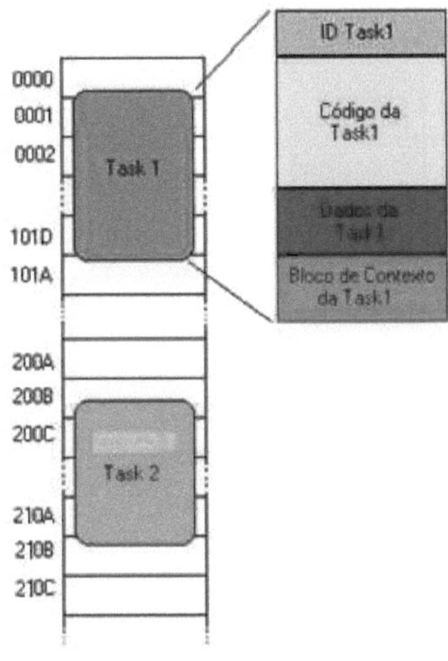

Figure 4: Distribution of tasks in memory

Source: Elaborated by the author (2013)

Once the body of each Task is outlined, an overview of the process as a whole can now be laid out according to figure 5

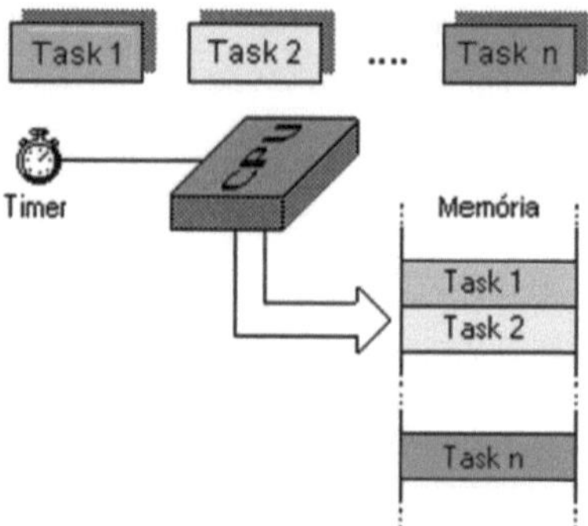

Figure 5: Process Overview

Source: Elaborated by the author (2013)

5.2. DYNAMIC OPERATION OF THE REAL-TIME SYSTEM

An RTC - Real Timer Clock, sends a clock pulse to the microcontroller's interrupt system, thus fixing the time to handle the tasks. It can also be observed that between one clock signal and the next, there is time to decide who will act on the use of the MPU.

All the while, the RTC sends a signal that generates an interrupt in the microcontroller. At each T cycle an interrupt occurs, and a special task activated at each T cycle, now called NTR - Real Time Core, determines which task should use the microcontroller and for how long (how many T cycles) to optimize the task scaling process .

In Figure 6 it can be seen that Task 2 occupied the MPU for two consecutive cycles.

This also leads to an important observation: in each cycle T two Tasks will occupy the MPU: the NTR and Task n that will be scaled. And this is repeated at each Cycle T .

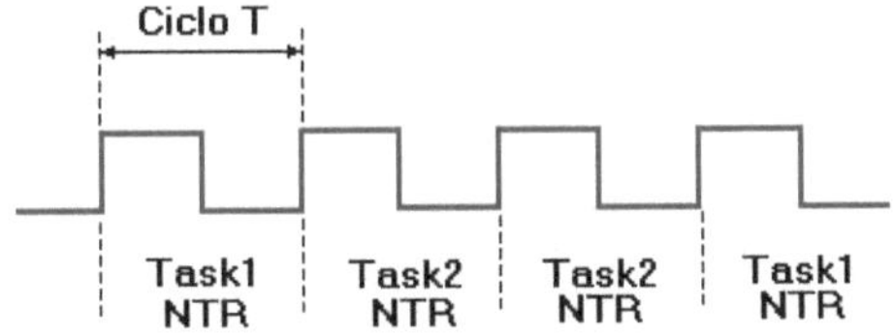

Figure 6: Task occupancy in time cycles

Source: Elaborated by the author (2013)

5.2.1. THE ESCALATION PROCESS

"One of the oldest, fairest, and , therefore widely used is called **round robin**" (TANENBAUM, 1992, p.45).   In this type of scheduler the task triggers the next and each task has an amount of time called **quantum**.   This suits the proposed system, because space is limited and each TASK has the code for "who will occupy the microcontroller in the sequence".

For this reason the proposed NTR does not work with the preemptive method (WIKIPEDIA 2013).

In the preemptive case, during the interrupt process the core determines which TASK will occupy the processor in the next interrupt cycle, so when leaving the NTR it has already set by priority the TASK that will occupy the processor in the next interrupt cycle. In the same way, the TASK that will occupy the microcontroller has already been set in the last interrupt cycle.

In the case of the NTR in this monograph the running task triggers the next task that will occupy the processor.

Although it is a maximum processor utilization system, it is an older real-time system. Even so, it is extremely functional in the case of low memory, which is this case.

5.3. THE CORE OF THE REAL-TIME SYSTEM - NTR

Each Task carries within it some essences that complement the Real Time concept.

This is a problem that deserves special treatment. Giving symmetric shares of time to tasks is not uncommon; Time Sharing systems use the concept of standard time quotas. The biggest drawback is that some tasks have associated with them a new characteristic that distinguishes these processes from all the others - the priority (TANENBAUM 1992).

Take for example simple tasks on a computer system, such as printing a file, and another that downloads a file from the Internet.

It is evident that the printing task is slower given its mechanical characteristics in contrast to the downloading task, which involves the Internet and high-speed serial protocol exchange. An accidental interruption of these protocols can lead to communication failure (time out). In turn, if the printer stops receiving characters, it stops printing. But, if both have equal and alternating shares of time, you can make both work satisfactorily.

But what if the elapsed time from the Internet is much longer ? That is, the time to download is much shorter than the time to print a single character. In other words, you can perform at least three times the downloading task for every once the printing task without monopolizing the downloading and without losing printing performance, all because the printer is much slower than the downloading process. The computer's operating system knows this and prioritizes the download.

The "prioritize" question must be incorporated into the NTR task so that it can define "who" should use the MPU in this T cycle and already schedule the next task without losing overall performance and without any task being able to monopolize the MPU; hence the importance of implementing the NTR task .

The most critical point of the debate centers around the fact that the Stack Pointer structure of the Intel family has remained unchanged since its first implementations.

As we will analyze later, this fact is of utmost importance in the implementation of a Real-Time system (software above all) because the stack is an indispensable means of handling tasks. Rigid Stack structures limit this implementation.

As the industrial process also becomes part of the system, and although this does not imply that the process defines the characteristics of the NTR, it must serve an industrial process and not just software tasks .

As the proposal is to involve the MPU in an industrial control, it is necessary to analyze some principles that involve the industrial process in order not to incur in some, whose service time is less than the interruption treatment time, which would cause the loss of the service point to the same as seen in figure 7. Note that the service request occurred at a time when the system was in interruption treatment of the NTR.

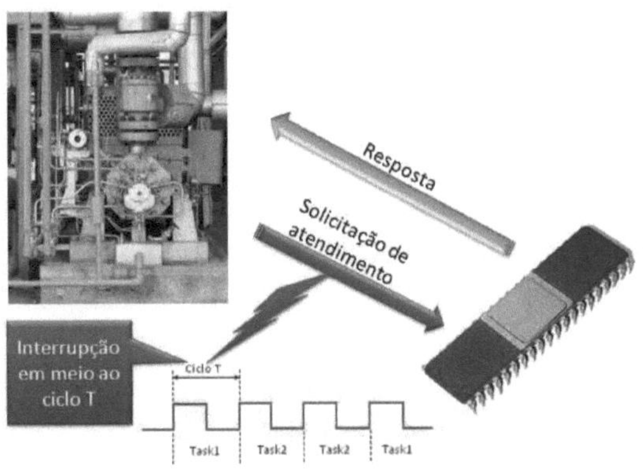

Figure 7: Loss of point of service

Source: Elaborated by the author (2013)

The concept of time becomes important in this environment because it provides a complete understanding of the very limits of the operating system. In theory there will be an interrupt every 1 mS. Considering that the internal clock is 1 MHz, the processor, being from the RISC family, has powerful instructions of only 1 cycle - for the most part - which means that it is capable of processing 1,000,000 instructions per second, or that it consumes 1x10-6 seconds in each instruction (1 µS).

This implies that the biggest problem would be in processes whose response times are much less than at least 100 µS, because the NTR also processes every 100 mS and has codes, which means that it consumes some time between every 1 mS (RTC timeout). In this way, processes with very fast response could compromise the performance of the core. Moreover, because it is a class B real-time system, it is not acceptable to just ignore the service request (interrupt request seen in Figure 7) and "memorize" this event in order to resume its treatment.

Following this line of reasoning a Real Time Operating System can be proposed respecting in particular the response time to events external to the process.

Since their inception, microcontrollers have had various interrupt levels as can be seen in the AT89S8253 datasheet from ATMEL© (p. 2) which are highlighted in figure 8 in red are pins 1,12,13,14 and 15 which cater for:

1....... Timer 2

12.....External Interruption 0

13.....External Interruption 1

14.....0

15.....1

And then there are the internal interrupts that can be generated by Timers 0, 1 and 2, and also the UART serial communication interrupt.

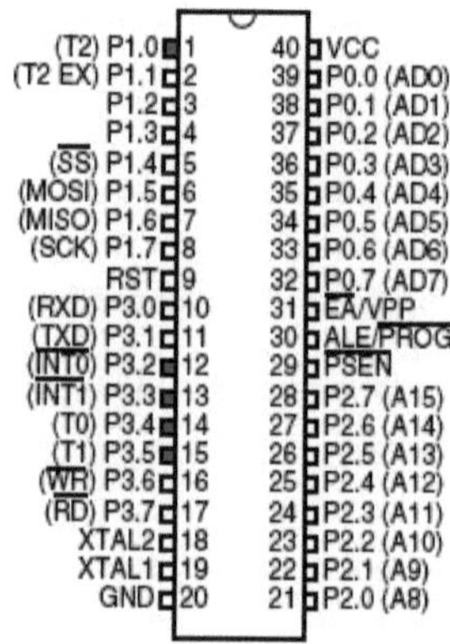

Figure 8: Pinout of the ATMEL AT89S8253

Source: ATMEL (2012)

According to the AT89S8253 datasheet from ATMEL© (p. 37) the programming area is located between 0000h and 2FFFh and corresponds to 12K program codes written in flashrom up to 10,000 times (p. 1).

Also respecting the existing interrupt vector at address 0000h as in Table 1.

Interrupt Source	Vector	Address
System Reset	RST or POR	0000H
External Interrupt 0	IE0	0003H
Timer 0 Overflow	TF0	000BH
External Interrupt 1	IE1	0013H
Timer 1 Overflow	TF1	001BH
Serial Port	IR or TI or SPIF	0023H

Table 1: Outage vector

Source: Elaborated by the author (2013)

Based on this one can think of a proposal in the form shown in figure 9.

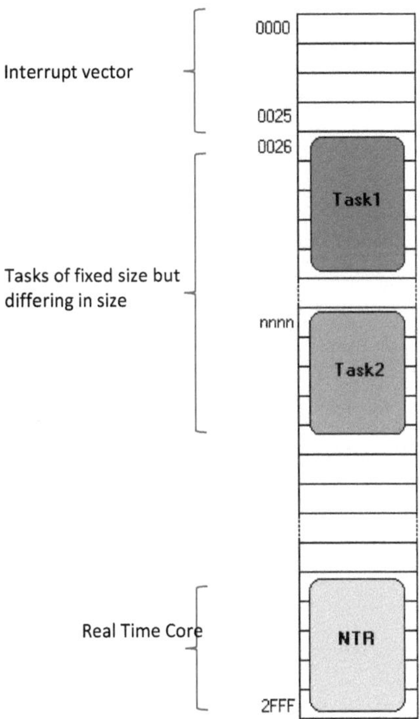

Figure 9: Operating system overview

Source: Elaborated by the author (2013)

And then the BCT can be established in the form of figure 10:

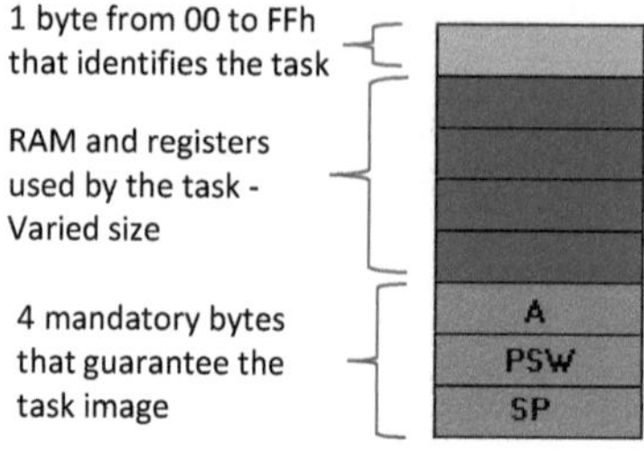

Figure 10: Detailed BCT

Source: Elaborated by the author (2013)

Due to the flexibility of the Stack Pointer it became simpler to build the NTR while avoiding control over the Program Counter register.

5.4. NTR SOFTWARE STRUCTURE

The following are the flowcharts relating to the NTR. Figure 11 represents the actions of the NTR at the time of interruption.

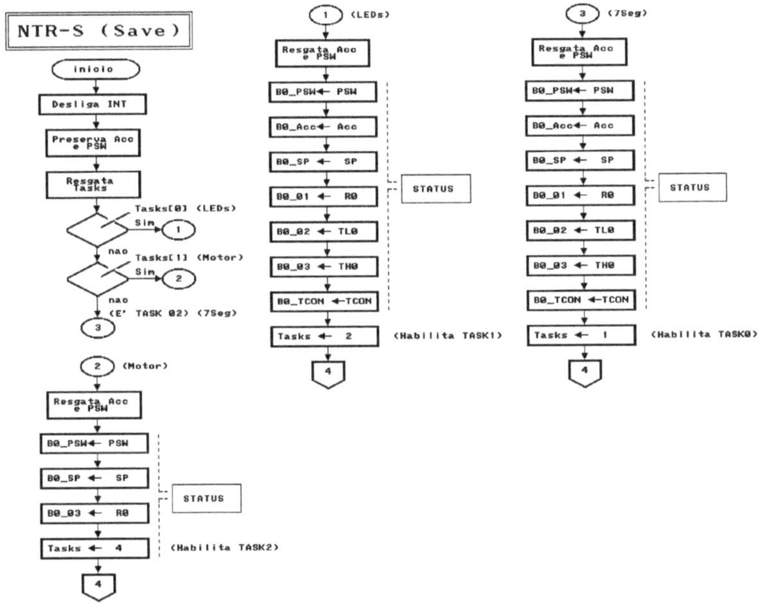

Figure 11: NTR Flowchart when entering an Outage

Source: Elaborated by the author (2013)

Here it is worth noting that according to the **round robin scheduler,** the TASKs themselves trigger the next TASK (take as an example, just above, the Tasks ⟵ 4 block)

Next in figure 12 is the return to the processor with the interrupts enabled.

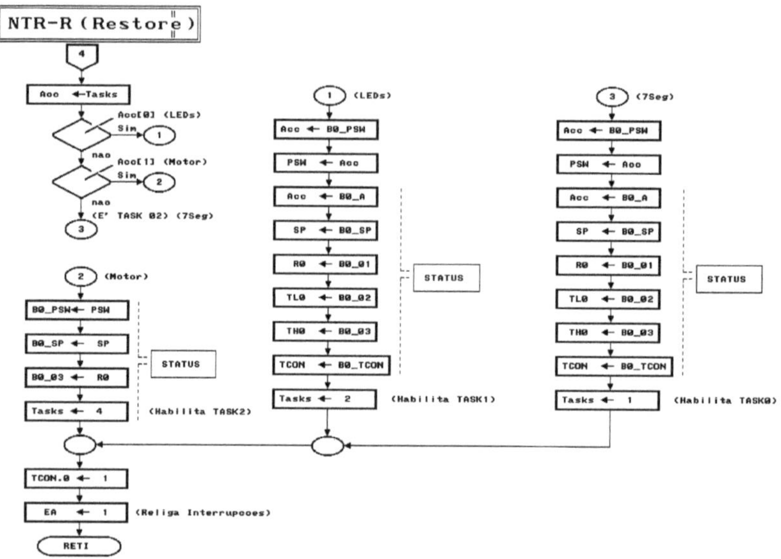

Figure 12: NTR Flowchart when exiting the interruption

Source: Elaborated by the author (2013)

5.5. PROPOSAL FOR TEST HARDWARE

For the development of the hardware tests we suggest the use of the PROTEUS simulator for its characteristic of allowing microcontroller program simulation. The proposed scheme for the tests is shown in figure 13.

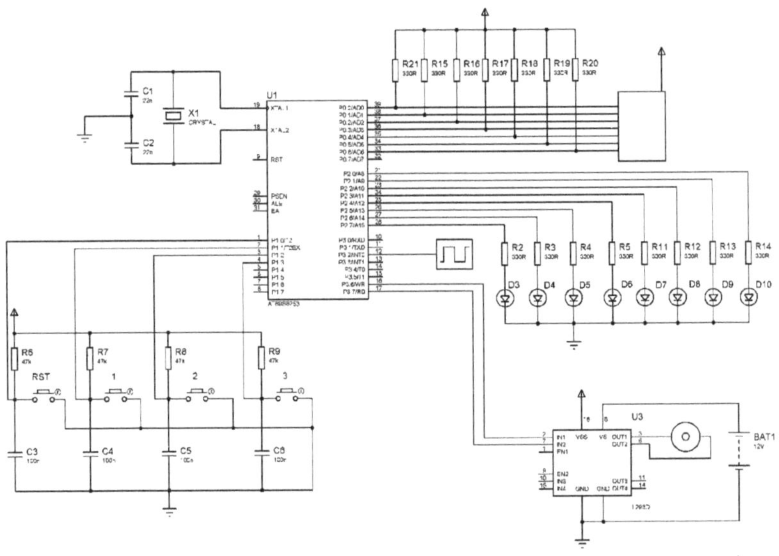

Figure 13: Proposed test circuit

Source: Elaborated by the author (2013)

As you can see, this circuit offers a 7-segment display, 7 LEDs, 4 buttons, and 1 DC motor as features, sufficient for several tasks under control.

The RTC generator, will be implemented by a circuit with the LM555 IC - a NATIONAL timer, configured to generate a 1 KHz square signal for an interrupt with 1 mS according to figure 14.

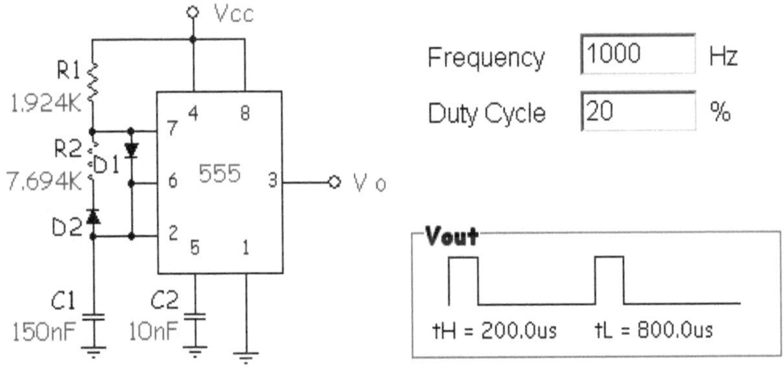

Figure 14: Circuit for generating 1 mS

Source: 555 etcetera version 1.4

Although the simulator does not offer absolutely accurate performance, it greatly speeds up the analysis of simple tests, and in the future it may be implemented in the AT89S8253 kit published at www.vargasp.com which can be seen in the picture on figure 15.

Figure 15: Real board for testing with AT89S8253

Source: Elaborated by the author (2013)

Starting from a proposal of executing TASKs in apparently simultaneous conditions (TIME-REAL) the suggested tasks would be triggered in sequence with a **quantum** (TANENBAUM, 1992, p.45) of 1 mS. During processing, the tasks will be triggered sequentially and cyclically as shown in Figure 16.

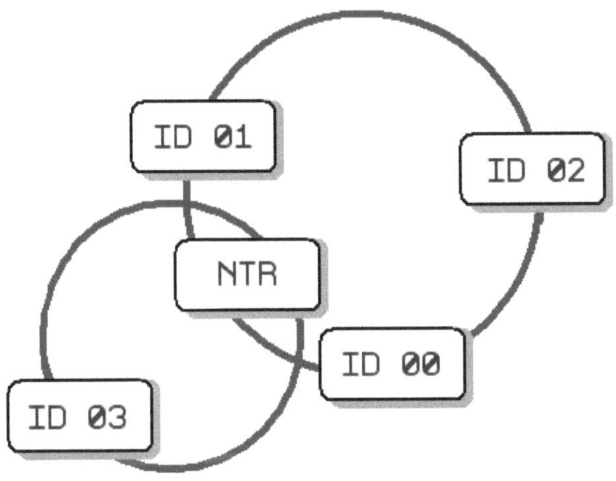

Figure 16: Interrelationship of TASKs

Source: Elaborated by the author (2014)

The tasks proposed for the test will be:

a) Count down from 9 to 0 and repeat the sequence (ID 02);

b) A led runs through the row of 8 leds from right to left and repeats this cycle (ID 00);

c) A DC motor accepts commands from buttons 1,2 and 3 in the following sequence:

    a. 1 for the engine;

    b. 2 turns the motor counterclockwise;

    c. 3 turns the motor clockwise

    (ID 01)

d) A timer generates times of 0.5 S (ID 03) to fulfill tasks a) and b).

Each TASK carries in its final code the code of the next TASK that will use the MPU after returning from the **round robin** interrupt (TANENBAUM).

Context switching is performed every 1 mS by the TASK NTR. This implies that each TASK uses one quantum and is replaced by the NTR by the next TASK that the core identified by the existing code in the interrupted task.

6. CONCLUDING REMARKS

The proposed NTR performed very well in simulations with Labcenter Electronics' proprietary PROTEUS software (1989-2009) Release 7.7 SP2 (Build 9089) with Advanced Simulation, which showed, at least visually, the "simultaneous" operation of the TASKs.

Since the beginning the proposal was to develop an RTC - Real Timer Clock system in process control equipment with microcontrollers and it was possible to meet this proposal .

It remains to study an industrial process in order to understand how a real-time system would work in this universe and also how to proceed to adapt to this reality.

Similarly, the study of safe latency time, even superficially will allow us to understand the possibility of creating a safe margin for the operating system to respond in Real Time to the quantities involved in the real process.

To develop the prototype of a Real-Time Operating System to serve a process and the local control of the devices involved, and further evaluate its performance against noise intolerances, timing errors - which usually occurs in process transitions with rapid variation - is a challenging and stimulating task.

In this test it was not yet possible to establish the handling of a real control process, but due to the stability presented it can be assumed that a simple process can be safely handled by the proposed system. The use of simple devices such as motor control and visual tasks demonstrates the capability of the System.

The most challenging point is timer sharing, because there is a loss of time between task exchanges. But considering that there are four active tasks, the time loss will be 3 mS until the interrupted timer task returns.

This gap will be the "Achilles heel" of the system. Processes that need to be serviced with more precision than this delay will not be supported. There is also the possibility of expanding the limits of the OS by reducing the RTC time (less than 1 mS), but this hypothesis has not yet been tested.

On top of all this, as a new generation of programmers is booming, just having the hope of offering a new programming technology - a controlled environment that frees up resources (Operating System) - is already enough for the original premise.

In the appendix is attached the source software developed in Assembly for the 8051 which was written with Jen's File Editor version 3.84 (free software), compiled with ASEN51 version 1.3 (free software) and tested with The 8051 machine version 1.0 Beta 3 (free software)

7. REFERENCES

FIGINI, G. **Industrial Electronics** 1.Ed. SÃO PAULO: HEMUS 1990

MAGALHÃES, M.F. **Software para tempo real** 1.Ed. CAMPINAS: EDITORA DA UNICAMP 1986

DORF, R.C. Sistemas de Controle **Modernos** 11.Ed. RIO DE JANEIRO: LTC 2009

BENTO,C.R. **Sistemas de Controle:Teoria e projetos** 1.Ed. SÃO PAULO: ÉRICA,1989

TANENBAUM, A.S. **Sistemas Operacionais Modernos** RIO DE JANEIRO: PRENTICE- HALL DO BRASIL, 1992

GUIMARÃES, M. P. **Introdução aos Sistemas Operacionais - ISO**, Técnico em Informática com habilitação em programação e desenvolvimento de sistemas, Salto, 2010

BBI - BIBLIOTECA BÁSICA INFORMÁTICA**Sistemas operacionais e software de base**,São Paulo:Ed. Século Futuro Ltda,1986, v.10

VALLE, J. C. The world's first electronic computer . 2010. Available at: **http://www.museudocomputador.com.br/historia_eniac.html** Accessed August 2013

MCCARTHY, J. Stanford University - Reminiscences on the history of time sharing. 1983. Disponível em:

http://www-formal.stanford.edu/jmc/history/timesharing/timesharing.html

INTEL CORPORATION. The Story of the Intel® 4004. 2013. Disponível em: **http://www.intel.com/content/www/us/en/history/museum-story-of-intel-4004.html**

ATMEL CORPORATION. Datasheet of the AT89S8253 from ATMEL©. Available at:

http://www.atmel.com/products/microcontrollers/8051architecture/default.aspx ?tab=documents

WIKIPEDIA - THE FREE ENCYCLOPEDIA - History of operating systems. 2013 Disponível em : **http://en.wikipedia.org/wiki/History_of_operating_systems**

WIKIPEDIA - THE FREEENCYCLOPEDIA-Preemptivity.2013

Available from: http://**pt.wikipedia.org/wiki/Preemptividade**

8. APPENDIX

Source program:

; --

; Program: NTR.asm

Date   : 23/11/2013

Author   : Prof. Vargas

The detailed description is in routine NTR

Timer0 is free to use and two tasks use it: ID00 ; and ID02 and therefore has different treatment.

; The SPs are respectively:

; ID00..... 20h

; ID01..... 27h

; ID02..... 2Ah

; And the Task locations are:

ID00 .....026h (Leds)

; ID01..... 040h (Engine)

ID02 .....071h (7 Sec)

ID03 .....0A9h (Timer05S)

; --

Definition of NTR variables and BCTs

;

;BCT_00

B0_ID   equ   50h

B0_01   equ   51h

B0_02   equ   52h

```
B0_03    equ    53h

B0_A     equ    55h

B0_PSW   equ    56h

B0_SP    equ    57h

B0_TCON  equ    58h


;BCT_01

B1_ID    equ    59h

B1_01    equ    5Ah

B1_02    equ    5Bh

B1_03    equ    5Ch

B1_A     equ    5Eh

B1_PSW   equ    5Fh

B1_SP    equ    60h


;BCT_02

B2_ID    equ    61h

B2_01    equ    62h

B2_02    equ    63h

B2_03    equ    64h

B2_A     equ    66h

B2_PSW   equ    67h

B2_SP    equ    68h

B2_TCON  equ    69h
```

```
Tasks     equ    6Ah   ;List of Tasks

Aux_00    equ    6Bh   ;Auxiliary for NTR

Aux_01    equ    6Ch   ;Auxiliary for NTR

Aux_Acc   equ    6Dh   ;Auxiliary for Acc

Aux_PSW   equ    6Eh   ;Auxiliary for PSW

control   equ    81h   ;hab. int 0

prior     equ    01h   ;high priority int0

typein    equ    01h   ;active in transition


;============

;   START

;============

    org    000

    ljmp   Start


    org    003h   ;Real Time Core

ljmp   NTR


Start:

    mov    Tasks,#00000001b   ; Active Task ID0

    mov    IE,#control

    mov    IP,#prior

    mov    TCON,#typein

;++++++++++++++++++++++++

    Initializing Tasks
```

;++++++++++++++++++++++++

; ID01..... 040h (Engine)

SP 27h

   mov   27h,#40h

   mov   28h,#00h

   mov   B1_SP,#28h

   ID02 .....071h (7 Sec)

SP   2Ah

mov   2Ah,#71h

   mov   2Bh,#00h

mov   B2_SP,#2Bh

ID03 0A9h(Timer05S)

;~~~~~~

Routine : Task1.asm (ID 00)

; Description:

This routine is part of an NTR test. It se-

The LED line is coupled to PORT P2

Records used:

R0, Acc, SP for Timer0

;

Subroutines used:

; time05S

;

In addition, SP needs only 4 bytes for

It will work correctly in this routine.

```
;~~~~~~~~~~~~~~~~~~~~~~~~~~~~~~~~~~~~~~~~~~~~~~~~~~~~~~~~~~

    org     026h
ID00:
    mov     SP,#20h     ;proper address of STACK
again:
    mov     P2,#00      ; Apg the LEDs
mov     R0,#09      ;Top of the countdown
    setb    P2.0        ;lights up the first
laco:
lcall    time05S
djnz     R0,prox
ljmp     again
prox:
    mov     A,P2
rl     A
    mov     P2,A
ljmp laco


;~~~~~~~~~~~~~~~~~~~~~~~~~~~~~~~~~~~~~~~~~~~~~~~~~~~~~~~~~~

Routine    : Task2.asm (ID 01)
; Description:
This routine is part of an NTR test. Manage
```

; the motor (On-OFF) by Button P1.2

Records used:

None.

;~~~~~~

```asm
        org     040h
ID01:
        mov     SP,#27h     ;proper address of STACK
        clr     P3.6        ;00-00.0000 stops motor
        clr     P3.7        ;00-00.0000 stops motor
other:
        jnb     P1.3,time   ;Time Button ?
        jnb     P1.2,anti   ;Anti-Timer Button ?
        jb      P1.1,another ;again
stop:
        jnb     P1.1,$      ;wait for the button to be released
        clr     P3.6
        clr     P3.7        ;On counterclockwise
        ljmp    other
anti:
        jnb     P1.2,$      ;wait for the button to be released
        setb    P3.6
        clr     P3.7        ;On counterclockwise
        ljmp    other
time:
        jnb     P1.3,$      ;wait for the button to be released
```

        clr   P3.6

        setb   P3.7   ;On counterclockwise

        ljmp   other

;~~~~~~

Routine   : Task3.asm (ID 02)

; Description:

This routine is part of an NTR test.

It is a countdown timer from 9 to 0 that decodes

; in a 7-segment display, in the form:

tos letter by letter by timing.

;   a   P0.0 = a

;   ---   P0.1 = b

; f | g | b   P0.2 = c

;   ---   P0.3 = d

; e | | c   P0.4 = e

;   ---   P0.5 = f

;   d   P0.6 = g

Each segment lights with level "0".

;

    0gfe dcba

; 9 = 0001 0000 ... 0x10

; 8 = 0000 0000 ... 0x00

; 7 = 0111 1000 ... 0x78

; 6 = 0000 0010 ... 0x02

; 5 = 0001 0010 ... 0x12

; 4 = 0001 1001 ... 0x19

; 3 = 0011 0000 ... 0x30

; 2 = 0010 0100 ... 0x24

; 1 = 0111 1001 ... 0x79

; 0 = 0100 0000 ... 0x40

; ------------------------

Records used:

None.

;

Subroutines used:

; time05S

;

;~~~~~~
;

```
    org    071h
ID02:
    mov    SP,#2Ah     ;proper address of STACK
    mov    P3,#00      ;00-00.0000 stops motor
    mov    30h,#10h    ;Write in RAM starting at 030h
    mov    31h,#00h
    mov    32h,#78h
    mov    33h,#02h
    mov    34h,#12h
    mov    35h,#19h
    mov    36h,#30h
```

```assembly
        mov     37h,#24h

        mov     38h,#79h

        mov     39h,#40h

princ:

        mov     R0,#30h     ;points to the first

proxy:

        mov     P0,@R0      ;sends to the display

    call    time05S

    inc     R0

    cjne    R0,#3Ah,proxi

    ljmp princ
```

;~~~~~~
;

Subroutine time05S.asm (ID 03)

; Author: Prof. Vargas

Date:07/19/03 17:05:08

The following routine is 0.5 S timer, and we get this

calculating 20 ms/(6/11.0592 MHz) = 36864.

Making 65535 - 36864 = 28671 or 0x6FFF.

Executing 25 x this value gives ~ 0.5 S

;

Records used:

Acc, TH0, TL0

;~~~~~~
;

```assembly
        org     0A9h
```

```
time05S:

    mov    Aux_00,Acc ;Release Acc

    mov    Acc,#25    ;counter of 25

    setb   PT0        ;priority 1

    mov    TMOD,#01   ;Timer 0 in mode1 16bit

cargo:

    mov    TH0,#06Fh

    mov    TL0,#0FFh

  setb   TR0        ;on counter 1

    jnb    TF0,$      ;wait for overflow

    clr    TR0        ;switches Timer0 off

    clr    TF0        ;Clear flag

    djnz   Acc,load

    mov    Acc,Aux_00

    ret


;-=-=-=-=-=-=-=-=-=-=-=-=-=-=-=-=-=-=-=-=-=-=-=-

Program : NTR.asm

Date    : 27/11/2013

; Description:

This is the Real-Time Core that manages the pro-

The structure is discussed in more detail in the following sections. Its structure is discussed
in

; details in the document RealTime.doc presented as

TCC at ESAB - Escolas Superior Aberta do Brasil, in

; Graduate course in Systems Engineering under
```

; oriented by Professor Caribe Zampirolli de Souza

;-=-   org   0C9h

NTR:

```
    clr    EA

    mov    Aux_Acc,Acc    ;Preserves Acc

mov    Aux_PSW,PSW        ; Preserves PSW

    mov    Acc,Tasks

jb     Acc.0,BCT00    Serial LED

jb     Acc. 1,BCT01     ;is ID 01 ... ENGINE

    jb     Acc.2,BCT02     ;is ID 02 ... 7Seg
```

; --

From here on the BCTs will be deployed

; --

BCT00:

```
    mov    Acc,Aux_Acc ;For order retrieves Acc

    mov    PSW,Aux_PSW ;For order retrieves PSW

mov    B0_PSW,PSW

    mov    B0_A,Acc

    mov    B0_SP,SP

    mov    B0_01,R0

    mov    B0_02,TL0

    mov    B0_03,TH0

mov    B0_TCON,TCON

    mov    Tasks,#02   ;Aim next task
```

```asm
        ljmp    restore
BCT01:
        mov     Acc,Aux_Acc ;In order to retrieve Acc
        mov     PSW,Aux_PSW ;In order to retrieve PSW
    mov     B1_PSW,PSW
        mov     B1_SP,SP
    mov     B1_03,R0
        mov     Tasks,#04   ;Aim next task
        ljmp    restore
BCT02:
        mov     Acc,Aux_Acc ;In order to retrieve Acc
        mov     PSW,Aux_PSW ;In order to retrieve PSW
    mov     B2_PSW,PSW
        mov     B2_A,Acc
        mov     B2_SP,SP
        mov     B2_01,R0
        mov     B2_02,TL0
        mov     B2_03,TH0
    mov     B2_TCON,TCON
        mov     Tasks,#01   ;Aim next task


restore:
        mov     Acc,Tasks
    jb      Acc. 0,Rec00    ;is ID 00 ... Serial LED
    jb      Acc. 1,Rec01    ;is ID 01 ... ENGINE
```

```asm
jb    Acc.2,Rec02    7Seg

Rec00:

    mov    Acc,B0_PSW

    mov    PSW,Acc

    mov    Acc,B0_A

    mov    SP,B0_SP

    mov    R0,B0_01

    mov    TL0,B0_02

    mov    TH0,B0_03

    mov    TCON,B0_TCON

ljmp end


Rec01:

    mov    Acc,B1_PSW

    mov    PSW,Acc

    mov    SP,B1_SP

mov    R0,B1_01

ljmp end


Rec02:

mov    Acc,B2_PSW

    mov    PSW,Acc

    mov    Acc,B2_A

    mov    SP,B2_SP
```

```
mov     R0,B2_01

  mov     TL0,B2_02

mov     TH0,B2_03

  mov     TCON,B2_TCON


end:

  setb    TCON.0     ;Maintains interrupt structure

  setb    EA

  reti

  end
```

I want morebooks!

Buy your books fast and straightforward online - at one of world's fastest growing online book stores! Environmentally sound due to Print-on-Demand technologies.

Buy your books online at
www.morebooks.shop

Kaufen Sie Ihre Bücher schnell und unkompliziert online – auf einer der am schnellsten wachsenden Buchhandelsplattformen weltweit! Dank Print-On-Demand umwelt- und ressourcenschonend produziert.

Bücher schneller online kaufen
www.morebooks.shop

KS OmniScriptum Publishing
Brivibas gatve 197
LV-1039 Riga, Latvia
Telefax: +371 686 204 55

info@omniscriptum.com
www.omniscriptum.com

Printed by Books on Demand GmbH, Norderstedt / Germany